MW01231643

Ninja Foodi Smart Xl Grill Cookbook For Beginners

The Complete Guide to The Innovative Ninja Foodi Smart Xl Grill Appliance With Tasty Indoor Grill And Air Fryer Savory Recipes

Lilla Marcus

Table of Contents

INTRODUCTION 8

CHAPTER 1: SIX METHODS OF NINJA FOODI XL SMART GRILL. 10

GRILL 10

AIR CRISP..10

BAKE 11

ROAST 11

DEHYDRATE 11

THE INSPIRATION BEHIND THIS COOKBOOK 11

WHAT MAKES THE NINJA FOODI SO GREAT? 12

MAKING THE MOST OF YOUR NINJA FOODI 12

NINJA FOODI SMART XL GRILL 14

CHAPTER 2: BREAKFAST RECIPES 16

1.   BACON AND EGG STUFFED PEPPERS 17

2.   BACON & SPINACH MUFFINS 19

3.   BUTTERNUT SQUASH WITH ITALIAN HERBS 21

4.   BAKED WESTERN OMELETS 23

5.   FLAVORFUL TURKEY JERKY 25

CHAPTER 3: MEAT RECIPES 28

6.   BEEF EMPANADAS..29

7.   AUTHENTIC KOREAN CHILI PORK 32

8.   BARBECUE JUICY PORK CHOPS..34

9.   BAKED RIGATONI WITH BEEF TOMATO SAUCE..36

10.   STRIP STEAK GRILLED NY WITH ASPARAGUS 39

11.   GRILLED CUMIN TENDERLOIN SPICED..41

CHAPTER 4: FISH RECIPES **44**

12. ALL-TIME FAVORITE CODES...45

13. CHILI LIME TILAPIA...47

14. LOVELY AIR FRIED SCALLOPS...49

15. LOVELY PANKO COD..50

16. SALMON PAPRIKA 52

CHAPTER 5: VEGETABLE RECIPES **54**

17. CASHEW STUFFED MUSHROOMS..55

18. CRUSTED BRUSSELS SPROUTS WITH SAGE..............................57

CHAPTER 6: APPETIZERS AND SNACKS RECIPES........................... **60**

19. CABBAGE AND PORK GYOZA...61

20. CHEESY POTATO TAQUITOS...63

21. BLT WITH GRILLED HEIRLOOM TOMATO..............................65

22. BROCCOLI BITES 67

23. ROSEMARY AND BAKED POTATOES..69

CHAPTER 7: DESSERTS RECIPES **72**

24. BANANA FRITTER...73

25. BLOOMIN' GRILLED APPLES..75

26. CHEESE AND HAM STUFFED BABY BELLA..............................77

27. NUTELLA CAKE..79

CHAPTER 8: MAIN RECIPES **82**

28. AIR FRIED LAMB'S CHOPS 83

29. DELICIOUS DONUTS IN NINJA FOODI SMART XL GRILL 85

30. FROZEN BARBECUE CHICKEN BREASTS...................................88

31. CHILI-RUBBED STEAK & BREAD SALAD 90

CHAPTER 9: SIDES RECIPES...**92**

32.   BUFFALO CHICKEN MEATBALLS...93

33.   CITRUS CARROTS...96

CHAPTER 10: POULTRY RECIPES.......................................**98**

34.   CRISPY CHICKEN STRIPS...99

35.   GARLIC CHICKEN POTATOES...101

36.   NINJA FOODI FRIED CHICKEN WITH SMASHED POTATOES AND

CORN   103

37.   TURKEY BURGERS WITH CHEDDAR AND ROASTED ONIONS 105

38.   BACON-WRAPPED TURKEY TENDERLOINS WITH HONEY BALSAMIC

CARROTS..108

39.   MAPLE-GLAZED CHICKEN WINGS.......................................111

40.   BREADED CHICKEN PICCATA...113

CONCLUSION **116**

Introduction

Ninja Foodi XL Grill Cookbook" introduces you to the Ninja Foodi XL grill and provides you with over 2000 healthy recipes created only for this grill. The book will show you how to prepare a variety of delicious dishes with this versatile grill.

This is the food processor that I have been waiting for since I started cooking. Its large capacity bowl and versatile blade assembly make it an ideal product to use for everyday cooking.

Foodi Smart XL Grill, the latest kitchen appliance by Ninja Foodi, is a food processor that can be used as a griller, slicer, mixer, and blender at homes.

Foodi Smart XL has a large processing bowl of 6.4 quarts capacity that can hold a lot of food for slicing or grilling. The bowl is large enough to make ten servings of coleslaw or salsa, and it is the perfect size for roasting a 3-pound chicken as well.

And the blade assembly can chop, slice shred, mix and blend.

The cookbook starts with an introduction to the Ninja Foodi XL grill. You will learn how to clean the grill, prepare it for use, and then go through the instructions for using this amazing kitchen appliance.

After reading "Ninja Foodi XL Grill Cookbook", you will be ready to make healthy and delicious dishes. You can use this book as a great reference guide for all your grill cooking needs. It can also be a significant learning experience for those who want to get inspired to cook new dishes or gain cooking skills.

When cooking at home, you want a cookbook that delivers. Every cookbook should be tailored to your specific needs, so why not designed for the Ninja Foodi XL Grill? The same team is written by Ninja Foodie XL Grill Cookbook's Ninja Foodie XL Grill Cookbook 1-2-3 series. The Ninja Foodi XL Grill Cookbook offers a practical approach to grilling that will help you get the most from your new grill.

Previous grills have either been too small or not easy to use. I wanted to create the perfect healthy alternative for my family, so I worked on creating a healthier way to cook and grill.

But my mission wasn't only to create a healthy way of cooking but to also make it easy for everyone.

With Ninja Foodi Smart XL Grill everything is easier, and you will be able to enjoy your favorite grilled food with less work and hassle.

While all of our cookbooks provide a great foundation for your grilling adventures, this one is specially designed for this recent addition to the Ninja Foodi XL Grill Cookbook family. We love our Ninja Foodi XL Grill, so we took extra time to make sure we offered the best possible guidance on its proper use.

The Ninja Foodi grill and the other grills differ in several ways. The enormous difference is that the Ninja Foodi Grill heats faster than other grills and cooks much more evenly. This is because the Ninja Foodi Smart XL grill is a solid core-less infrared grill. It uses ceramic infrared burners, which are in a cylinder inside the grill, therefore there are no gaps between the heating elements (unlike most electric grills).

Whether you are a first-time griller or a seasoned pro, The Ninja Foodie XL Grill Cookbook delivers the information you need to ensure that your time spent on the grill will reward and pleasurable.

CHAPTER 1:

Six Methods of Ninja Foodi XL Smart Grill

N ow that you have a basic idea of what the Ninja Foodi Smart XL Grill is let's look at the core functions and buttons you should know about. Remember that you have five different cooking types that you can do using your Ninja Foodi Grill.

Grill

At its heart, the Ninja Foodi Smart XL Grill is an indoor grill, so to unlock its full potential, you must understand how the grill function of the appliance works. Let me break it down to you.

Now understand that each set of the Grill is specifically designed for fresh food.

But regardless of which function you choose, the first step for you will always be:

- Place your cooking pot and grill grate in the Ninja Foodi.'
- Let it pre-heat
- Then add your food

The next thing would be to select the Grill function and choose the Grill Temperature. Here you have 4 settings to choose from.

- **Low:** This mode is perfect for bacon and sausages.
- **Medium:** This is perfect for frozen meats or marinated meats.
- **High:** This mode is perfect for steaks, chicken, and burgers.
- **Max:** This is perfect for vegetables, fruits, fresh and frozen seafood, and pizza.

Air Crisp

The Air Crisp mode will help you achieve a very crispy and crunchy golden-brown finish to your food. Using the Air Crisp mode combined with the crisper basket is the perfect combination to cook frozen foods such as french fries, onion rings, and chicken nuggets. Air Crisp is also amazing for Brussels sprouts and other fresh vegetables. Just always shake the crisper basket once or twice to ensure even cooking.

Bake

As mentioned earlier, the Ninja Foodi Smart XL Grill is essentially a mini convection oven. All you need to bake bread, cakes, pies, and other sweet treats is a Cooking Pot and this function. The Pre-heat time for the Bake mode is just 3 minutes.

Roast

The Roast function is used to make everything from slow-roasted pot roast to appetizers to casual sides. Large protein pieces can be put directly in your Ninja Foodi Smart XL Grill and roasted using this function. You can further make this mode more effective by using a Roasting Rack accessory.

Dehydrate

Dehydrators are pretty expensive and take a lot of space in your kitchen. Luckily, you can very easily dehydrate fruits, meats, vegetables, herbs, etc., using just your Ninja Foodi Grill!

The Inspiration Behind This Cookbook

One of my all-time favorite foods is Beef Stew. It's a great meal to batch cook for those busy nights, but it's also what I make for my kids when they're sick. Beef stew is not only hearty and delicious, but it reminds me of my childhood in a way that could bring me to tears. Now, before my Ninja Foodi... Let me tell you how I used to make Beef Stew. First, I would pat dry the beef cubes and season them - this step is a no brainer. Next, I would heat a frying pan on high with some oil and slowly sear the beef, in batches so I didn't overcrowd the pan. It takes a long time and produces a lot of smoke, not to mention, using a lot of oil. Next, I would fill my slow cooker with stock and vegetables. This worked great but took all day to cook and created a lot of dishes to clean.

With the Ninja Foodi, I can sear, simmer, roast, and braise all in one easy-to-clean appliance. The pre-programmed buttons make it so easy, even my kids can make beef stew in it now! This is one of the tabletop appliances on the market that gets hot enough to sear meat properly, so the first thing I made with my Ninja Foodi was beef stew.

What Makes the Ninja Foodi so Great?

Authorization strolls you through how I make beef stew since getting my Ninja Foodi. I open a package of meat, season it, and add it to the Ninja foodi and set it to "sear." In minutes, the temperature has reached 500F so I set a timer after placing the lid on (so there's virtually no smoke at all,) and then come back when the timer has gone off to add the stock and fresh veggies… And voila! In just one hour I have tender, flavorful, juicy, hearty, healthy beef stew!

But it's more than just beef stew! I use my Ninja Foodi for just about everything now, which is why I wanted to create this cookbook (with more than 500 recipes!) to show you how you too can revolutionize the way you cook. You and your family will save time and be healthier in the end - it's really a win-win! (You might also end up feeling like a world-class chef in the end, because everything in this book is so tasty!)

Along with saving money on my energy bill and saving me tons of time around dinner time, this appliance also helped make me and my family healthier! I used to add a lot of oil to the surface of meat before cooking, to prevent it from sticking. I was fed up with losing half a chicken breast on the barbeque so then I started baking them, which didn't offer a lot of flavors. I also used a lot of oil on things like grilled bread, fish, or vegetables. But with the air crisp setting on this machine, you don't need to use any oil whatsoever… which has had an incredible impact on my health. If you're not concerned about oil, this machine will still allow you to enjoy more of the foods that fit into your meal plan – for keto or paleo diets, the Ninja Foodi is a great addition to your kitchen, because of how conveniently you can cook such a variety of proteins.

Making the Most of Your Ninja Foodi

The Ninja Foodi has 6 function buttons which completely replaced my toaster, toaster oven, deep fryer, oven, stovetop, microwave, and even my outdoor barbeque! With this device, I can roast a chicken, a whole fish, or any of my favorite oven meals. I can quickly heat up a piece of pizza or toast. I can air crisp chicken wings or fish sticks for the kids. I can bake a cake or fresh bread. I can dehydrate apple chips or kale chips. I can broil garlic bread or grilled cheese. And probably most impressively… I can grill with no smoke or fire hazards year-round indoors!! Now you try to name an appliance that can do all of that!?!?!

Now you may be wondering – "But is this thing really as good as my barbeque?" The answer is YES and once you try just a few of the recipes from this cook, you will see for yourself. So far, I have grilled everything from shrimp skewers to corn on the cob, to loaded baked potatoes, to hot dogs and yes, even the perfect medium-rare steak. The Ninja Foodi comes with a thermometer probe that is inserted into the center of a seasoned steak, to alert you when it's reached your desire doneness. Once the internal temperature of the steak reaches that temperature, you open the lid and have the perfectly cooked dinner. It really is that easy! Alongside your steak, you can also enjoy perfectly roasted vegetables and potatoes, and you can even enjoy a fresh-baked apple pie for dessert… all from your Ninja Foodi!

One of the finest parts of this machine though is that it reaches a temperature of 500F – this is almost unheard of for a tabletop interior grill. This high temperature allows me to properly sear my food (especially steaks, chicken, or fish) and really allows it to get those tasty grill marks. But this device does more than just sear, as I've told you… because of its unique cyclonic technology, it also circulates the air around your food continuously, which cooks food perfectly, every time.

Ninja Foodi Smart XL Grill

Characteristics	Ninja Foodi AG301 Grill	Ninja Foodi Smart XL Grill
Cooking programs	There are five cook programs. Grill, Air crisp, Bake, Roast, and Dehydrate.	There are six cook programs. Broil, Dehydrate, Air crisp, Roast, Bake, and Grill.
Smart temperature probe	Absent. You have to rely a bit on guesswork to attain that perfect doneness.	Dual sensor Present. To continuously monitor the temperature accuracy for even more perfect doneness. Multi-task away since it cancels the need to watch over the food.
Smart cook system	Absent. Requires frequent checks and guesswork for satisfactory results.	Present. With 4 smart protein settings and 9 customizable doneness levels, all the work is done to input the required setting. Just wait for your food to cook. You could be busy doing your laundry while you cook.
Weight	20 pounds	27.5 pounds
Dimension (L×W×H) inches	12.5 ×16.88×10.59 inches.	18.8 x 17.7 x 14 inches. Therefore, this is the larger option for large-sized family dishes and 50% more grilling space.

CHAPTER 2:

Breakfast Recipes

1. Bacon and Egg Stuffed Peppers

Preparation time: 10 minutes

Cooking time: 15 minutes

Servings: 4

Ingredients:

- 1 cup shredded Cheddar cheese

- 4 slices bacon, cooked and chopped

- 4 bell peppers, seeded and tops removed

- 4 large eggs

- Sea salt, to taste

- Freshly ground black pepper, to taste

- Chopped fresh parsley, for garnish

Directions:

1. Pull-out the Crisper Basket and adjust the hood. Choose AIR CRISP set the temperature to 390°F (199°C) and set the time to 15 minutes. Select START/STOP to begin preheating.

2. Meanwhile, divide the cheese and bacon between the bell peppers. Crack one of the eggs into each bell pepper, and season with salt and pepper.

3. When the unit toots to indicate it has preheated, place each bell pepper in the basket. Close the hood and AIR CRISP for 10 to 15 minutes, until the egg whites are cooked, and the yolks are slightly runny.

4. Remove the peppers from the basket, garnish with parsley, and serve.

Nutrition:

- Calories: 460

- Fat: 20 g

- Saturated Fat: 5 g

- Carbohydrates: 26 g

- Fiber: 3 g

- Sodium: 126 mg

- Protein: 28 g

2. Bacon & Spinach Muffins

Preparation Time: 10 minutes

Cooking Time: 17 minutes

Servings: 6

Ingredients:

- 6 eggs

- ½ cup milk

- Salt and black pepper to taste

- 1 cup fresh spinach, chopped

- 4 cooked bacon slices, crumbled

Directions:

1. In a dish, enhance the eggs, milk, salt, and black pepper and beat until well combined.

2. Add the spinach and stir to combine.

3. Divide the spinach mixture into 6 greased cups of an egg bite mold evenly.

4. Place the "Crisper Basket" in the pot of Ninja Foodi Grill.

5. Close the Ninja Foodi Grill by the lid and select "Air Crisp".

6. Set the temperature to 325 degrees F to pre-heat.

7. Choose "Start" to pre-heat.

8. When the display shows "Add Food," open the lid and place the muffin egg bite mold into the "Crisper Basket".

9. Close the Ninja Foodi Grill with a lid and set the time for 17 minutes.

10. Press "Start/Stop" to cook.

11. When the cooking time is completed, press "Start/Stop" to stop cooking and open the lid.

12. Place the muffin molds onto a wire rack to cool for about 5 minutes.

13. Carefully invert the muffins onto a platter and top with bacon pieces

14. Serve warm.

Nutrition:

- Calories: 179 Fat: 12.9 g

- Saturated Fat: 4.3 g

- Carbohydrates: 1.8 g

- Sugar: 1.3 g

Protein: 13.5 g

3. Butternut Squash with Italian Herbs

Preparation time: 5–10 minutes

Cooking time: 16 minutes

Servings: 4

Ingredients:

- 1 intermediate butternut squash, peeled, seeded, and cut into 1/2-inch slices

- 1 tsp. thyme, dried

- 1 tbsp. olive oil

- 1 1/2 tsp. oregano, dried

- 1/4 tsp. black pepper

- 1/2 tsp. salt

Directions:

1. Enhance all the ingredients into a mixing bowl and mix it.

2. Preheat your Ninja Foodi by pressing the GRILL option and setting it to MED.

3. Set the timer to 16 minutes.

4. Allow it to preheat until you hear a beep.

5. Arrange squash slices over the grill grate.

6. Cook for 8 minutes.

7. Flip them and cook for 8 minutes more.

8. Serve and enjoy!

Nutrition:

- Calories: 238

- Fat: 12 g.

- Saturated Fat: 2 g.

- Carbohydrates: 36 g.

- Fiber: 3 g.

- Sodium: 128 mg.

- Protein: 15 g.

4. Baked Western Omelets

Preparation time: 10 minutes.

Cooking time: 35 minutes.

Servings: 10

Ingredients:

- 10 eggs

- 1/3 cup milk

- Salt and pepper to taste

- 1–1/2 cup shredded Cheddar cheese

- 1–1/2 cup cooked ham, diced

- 1/2 cup red bell pepper, diced

- 1/34 cup green bell pepper, diced

Directions:

- Preheat the Ninja Foodi Smart XL by closing the crisping lid and selecting the bake button.

- Set the time to 5 minutes at 315°F.

- Meanwhile, take a mixing bowl and whisk together eggs, milk, salt, and pepper.

- Then add cheese, ham, red bell pepper, and green bell pepper.

- Mix all the ingredients.

- Generously grease the bottom of the Ninja Foodi Smart XL baking pan with oil spray.

- Pour egg mixture into the pan.

- Place the rack inside Ninja Foodi and put the pan on top.

- Lock the Ninja Foodi and select bake. Set temperate to 315°F for 35 minutes.

- Select start. Once the omelet is ready, serve and enjoy.

Nutrition

- Calories 137

- Fat 9.5g

- Carbohydrate 1.9g

- Dietary fibre 0.3g

- Protein 10.9g

5. Flavorful Turkey Jerky

Preparation time: 15 minutes.

Cooking time: 6 hours.

Servings: 4

Ingredients:

- 1 pound turkey tenderloins, trimmed fat and sliced ¼ inch thick

- ½ teaspoon liquid smoke

- 1 teaspoon black pepper

- 2 tablespoons brown sugar

- 2 teaspoons Worcestershire sauce

- ¼ cup soy sauce

- ½ cup water

- ¼ teaspoon Garlic powder

- ¼ teaspoon onion powder

Directions:

1. Combine onion powder, liquid smoke, pepper, sugar, Worcestershire sauce, soy sauce, water, and garlic powder. Stir until seasoning dissolves.

2. Add meat slices and mix until well coated. Cover bowl tightly and refrigerate overnight.

3. Spray dehydrator racks with cooking spray.

4. Remove marinated meat slices from marinade and shake off excess liquid. Arrange meat slices on dehydrator racks.

5. Arrange a dehydrator tray according to the manufacturer's instructions and dry at 145°F/63°C.

6. Turn on the Ninja Foodi Smart XL Grill and press the dehydrate button set time to 5–6 hours.

7. Let it cool jerky for 5–10 minutes, then store in a container.

Nutrition:

- **Calories:** 151

- **Total fat:** 1.5g

- **Protein:** 29.2g

- **Carbs:** 6.7g

- **Fiber:** 0.3g

- **Sugar:** 5.2g

CHAPTER 3:

Meat Recipes

6. Beef Empanadas

Preparation time: 15 minutes

Cooking time: 23 minutes

Servings: 2

Ingredients:

- 1 tablespoon extra-virgin olive oil

- ½ small white onion, finely chopped

- ¼ pound 80% lean ground beef

- 1 garlic clove, minced

- 6 green olives, pitted and chopped

- ¼ teaspoon paprika

- ¼ teaspoon ground cumin

- 1/8 teaspoon ground cinnamon

- 2 small tomatoes, chopped

- 8 square gyoza wrappers

- 1 egg, beaten

Directions:

1. Choice Sear/Sauté and fix it to Medium-High. Choice Start/Stop to begin. Let the pot heat for 5 minutes.

2. Put the oil, onion, ground beef, and garlic in the preheated pot and cook for 5 minutes, stirring occasionally.

3. Stir in the olives, paprika, cumin, and cinnamon and cook for an additional 3 minutes. Enhance the tomatoes and prepare for 1 minute more.

4. Carefully remove the beef mixture from the pot.

5. Place the Cook & Crisp Basket in the pot. Close the Crisping Lid. Preheat the unit by picking Air Crisp, set the temperature to 400°F and setting the time to 5 minutes.

6. While the Ninja® Foodi™ is preheating, arrange the gyoza wrappers on a flat surface. Place 1 to 2 tablespoons of the beef mixture in the center of each wrapper. Brush the wrapper's edges with the egg and carefully fold in half to form a triangle, pinching the edges together to seal them.

7. Arrange 4 empanadas in a single layer in the preheated Cook & Crisp™ Basket.

8. Adjust the Crisping Lid. Choice Air Crisp fix the temperature to 400°F and set the time to 7 minutes. Choice Start/Stop to begin. When cooking is complete, remove the empanadas from the basket and transfer them to a plate.

9. Repeat steps 7 and 8 with the remaining empanadas.

10. **TIP**: Experiment with different flavors for your empanadas by adding vegetables like mushrooms or potatoes or additional proteins like chorizo or diced Hard-boiled Eggs.

Nutrition:

- Calories: 394

- Total fat: 23 g

- Saturated fat: 6 g

- Cholesterol: 148 mg

- Sodium: 507 mg

- Carbohydrates: 30 g

- Fiber: 3 g

- Protein: 18 g

7. Authentic Korean Chili Pork

Preparation time: 10 minute

Cooking time: 8 minutes

Servings: 4

Ingredients:

- 2 lbs. pork, cut into 1/8-inch slices

- 5 garlic cloves, minced

- 3 tbsp. green onion, minced

- 1 yellow onion, sliced

- 1/2 cup soy sauce

- 1/2 cup brown sugar

- 3 tbsp. Korean Red Chili Paste

- 2 tbsp. sesame seeds

- 3 tsp. black pepper

- Red pepper flakes

Directions:

1. Take a zip bag and add listed ingredients, shake well and let it chill for 6–8 hours.

2. Pre-heat Ninja Foodi by demanding the GRILL option and situation it to MED and timer to 8 minutes.

3. Let it pre-heat till you hear a beep.

4. Arrange sliced pork over grill grate, lock the lid and cook for 4 minutes.

5. Flip pork and cook for 4 minutes more, serve warm and enjoy with some chopped lettuce.

Nutrition:

- Calories: 620

- Carbohydrates: 29 g.

- Fat: 31 g.

- Protein: 58 g.

8. Barbecue Juicy Pork Chops

Preparation time: 10 minutes.

Cooking time: 12 minutes.

Ready in about: 100 minutes.

Servings: 4

Ingredients:

- 4 bone-in pork chops

- 1(½) cups chicken broth

- 1 tablespoon freshly ground black pepper

- 1 tablespoon olive oil

- 4 tablespoons barbecue sauce

- 3 tablespoons brown sugar

- 1 tablespoon salt 1(½) tablespoon smoked paprika

- 2 teaspoon garlic powder

Directions:

- Preheat the Ninja Foodi Smart XL Grill for about 8 minutes. In a prepared small bowl, mix the brown sugar, salt, paprika, garlic powder, and black pepper. Put seasonings on both sides of the pork with the rub. Heat the oil in the preheated pot and sear the pork chops, one at a time, on both sides, about 5 minutes per chop. Set aside.

- Pour the chicken broth into a pot, and with a wooden spoon, scrape the bottom of the pot of any browned bits. Place the crisping basket in the upper position of the pot. Put the pork chops in the basket and brush with 2 tablespoons of barbecue sauce.

- Seal the lid, set it to high. Set the time to 5 minutes, then Choose start/stop to begin cooking. When the timer is done, perform a natural pressure release for 10 minutes, then a quick pressure release, and carefully open the lid.

- Apply the remaining barbecue sauce on both sides of the pork and close the crisping lid. Choose broil and set the time to 3 minutes. Press start/stop to begin. When ready, check for your desired crispiness and remove the pork from the basket.

Nutrition:

- Energy (calories): 565 Protein: 60.41g Fat: 27.41g

- Carbohydrates: 16.11g

9. Baked Rigatoni with Beef Tomato Sauce

Preparation time: 20 minutes.

Cooking time: 15 minutes.

Servings: 8

Ingredients:

1. 2 pounds ground beef

- 2(24-ounces) cans of tomato sauce

- 16-ounces dry rigatoni

- 1 cup cottage cheese

- 1 cup shredded Mozzarella cheese

- ½ cup chopped fresh parsley

- 1 cup of water

- 1 cup dry red wine

- 1 tablespoon butter

- ½ teaspoon garlic powder ½ teaspoon salt

- 1 Bell pepper, seeded and chopped

Directions:

- Preheat the Ninja Foodi Smart XL Grill. Melt the butter, add the beef and cook for 5 minutes, or until browned and cooked well. Stir in the tomato sauce, wine, water, and rigatoni; season with garlic powder and salt.

- Close the Ninja Foodi, set to low and set the time to 2 minutes. Choose start/stop to begin cooking.

- When the timer is done, perform a natural pressure release for 10 minutes, then carefully open the lid. Stir in the cottage cheese and evenly sprinkle the top of the pasta with the mozzarella cheese. Close the crisping lid.

- Choose broil and set the time to 3 minutes. Choose start/stop to begin. Cook for 3 minutes, or until the cheese has melted, slightly browned, and bubbly. Garnish with the parsley and serve immediately.

- Spoon the mixture filling into the bell peppers to the brim. Clean the inner pot with a paper towel and return the pot to the base. Pour 1 cup of water into the pool and fix the pot's rack in the lower position. Put the peppers on the stand and cover the tops loosely with a piece of foil.

- Close the lid, set to seal. Adjust the settings to high and the time to 12 minutes. Press start.

- After cooking, perform a quick pressure release and carefully open the lid. Get the foil from the top of the peppers and sprinkle the remaining ½ cup of cheese on the peppers.

- Close the crisping lid; choose broil, adjust the time to 5 minutes, and press Start to broil the cheese. After 4 minutes, open the cover and check the peppers.

- The cheese should have melted and browned a bit. If it is not yet, close the lid and continue cooking. Let the peppers cool for several minutes before serving.

Nutrition:

- **Energy (calories):** 744

- **Protein:** 45.22g **Fat:** 60.72g

Carbohydrates: 10.01g

10. Strip Steak grilled NY with Asparagus

Preparation Time: 10 minutes

Cooking Time: 12 minutes

Servings: 4

Ingredients:

- Black pepper ground, as desired.

- 2 spoonfuls of canola oil, divided.

- As needed, kosher salt

- 2 New York strip steaks not cooked (14-16 ounces).

- 1 asparagus bunch, trimmed

Directions:

1. Brush each steak in a 1/2 tbsp. of canola oil on each side and season as desired with salt and pepper. Place the remaining canola oil on the asparagus and season with salt and pepper as desired.

2. Install a grill in the device and close the hood grill. Select Grill, set High temperature and set time to 12 minutes. To start preheating, click Start/stop.

3. Put steaks on the grill of Ninja Foodi Smart XL and press them down to maximize grill marks. Open the hood for 4 minutes and cook.

4. Flip steaks after 4 minutes. Open the cap and continue to cook until the internal temperature exceeds 125 ° F. for four more minutes.

5. Get steaks from the grill and let them stand for 5 minutes, and start cooking while resting at a food-safe temperature. To ensure a healthy food temperature, using a cooking thermometer.

6. While the steaks rest, grill the asparagus. Steam the hood for 4 minutes.

7. Slice steaks and serve with asparagus when cooked.

Nutrition:

- Calories: 127

- Protein: 24.74 g

- Fat: 2.9 g

- Carbohydrates: 0.37 g

11.   Grilled Cumin Tenderloin Spiced

Preparation Time: 5 minutes

Cooking Time: 25 minutes

Servings: 6

Ingredients:

- 1/4 tea cubicle black pepper

- 1 tsp. of powdered garlic

- 1 tsp. of powdered chilli

- 1/2 square meters of cumin

- 1 kosher salt tbsp.

- 1/2 tsp. of peppers

- 1 pork tenderloin, approximately 18 oz.

Directions:

1. Combine the spices and season all over the tenderloin.

2. Preheat Ninja Foodi Smart XL to Grill or select Broiler.

3. Grill the grill or fried tenderloin, covered on each side for 5 minutes, then switch to indirect warmth while grilling, cover the grill and simmer for 10 to 12 minutes, turning halfway, to 145 °F. (total approximately 22 to 25 minutes) in an instant-

read thermometer mounted in the central position. Add more time for thicker tenderloin.

4. Let the pork rest approximately 5 minutes before slicing.

Nutrition:

- Calories: 178

- Protein: 23.83 g

- Fat: 8.11 g

- Carbohydrates: 0.91 g

CHAPTER 4:

Fish Recipes

12.   All-Time Favorite Codes

Preparation time: 5 minutes

Cooking time: 8 minutes

Servings: 4

Ingredients:

- 4 garlic cloves, minced

- 2 teaspoons coconut aminos

- ¼ cup butter

- 6 whole eggs

- 2 small onions, chopped

- 3 (4 ounces each) skinless codfish fillets, cut into rectangular pieces

- 2 green chilies, chopped

- Salt and pepper to taste

Directions:

1. Take a shallow dish and add all ingredients except cod. Beat the mixture well

2. Dip each fillet into the mixture and keep it on the side

3. Transfer prepared fillets to your Ninja Foodi Crisping basket and transfer basket to Pot

4. Lock Crisping lid and cook on "Air Crisp" mode for 8 minutes at 330 degrees F. Serve and enjoy!

Nutrition:

- Calories: 246

- Fat: 7.4 g

- Saturated Fat: 4.6 g

- Carbohydrates: 9.4 g

- Fiber: 2.7 g

- Sodium: 353 mg

Protein: 37.2 g

13.   Chili Lime Tilapia

Preparation time: 10 minutes

Cooking time: 22 minutes

Servings: 4

Ingredients:

- 1 lb. tilapia fillets

- 1 cup panko crumbs

- 1/2 cup flour

- Salt and black pepper to taste

- 1 lime juice

- 1 tbsp. chili powder

- 2 eggs

Directions:

1. Select the GRILL button on the Ninja Foodi Smart XL Grill and regulate Medium settings for 10 minutes.

2. Mingle the crumbs with salt, chili powder, and black pepper in a bowl.

3. Place flour in one bowl and whip egg in another bowl.

4. Dredge the fillets in the flour, then dip in the egg.

5. Cover with the panko mixture and arrange the fillets in the Ninja Foodi when it displays ADD FOOD.

6. Grill for about 10 minutes, tossing the fillets once in between.

7. Dole out the fillets in a platter and shower with lime juice to serve.

Serving suggestions: Roasted potatoes make a great side for Chili Lime Tilapia.

Variation tip: If you want a gluten-free option, then use pork rinds instead of breadcrumbs.

Nutrition:

- Calories: 327

- Fat: 3.5 g.

- Sat. Fat: 0.5 g.

- Carbohydrates: 33.6 g.

- Fiber: 0.4 g.

- Sugar: 9.2 g.

- Protein: 24.5 g.

14.   Lovely Air Fried Scallops

Preparation time: 5 minutes

Cooking time: 5 minutes **Servings:** 4

Ingredients:

- 12 scallops 3 tablespoons olive oil

- Salt and pepper to taste

Directions:

1. Gently rub scallops with salt, pepper, and oil.

2. Transfer to your Ninja Foodie's insert and place the insert in your Foodi.

3. Lock the Air Crisping lid and cook for 4 minutes at 390 degrees F.

4. Half through, give them a nice flip, and keep cooking. Serve warm and enjoy!

Nutrition:

- Calories: 246 Fat: 7.4 g Saturated Fat: 4.6 g

- Carbohydrates: 9.4 g Fiber: 2.7 g

- Sodium: 353 mg Protein: 37.2 g

15.   Lovely Panko Cod

Preparation time: 10 min

Cooking time: 27-29 min

Servings: 4

Ingredients:

- 2 uncooked cod fillets, 6 ounces each

- 3 teaspoons kosher salt

- ¾ cup panko breadcrumbs

- 2 tablespoons butter, melted

- ¼ cup fresh parsley, minced

- 1 lemon. Zested and juiced

Directions:

1. Pre-heat your Ninja Foodi at 390 degrees F and place the Air Crisper basket inside.

2. Season cod and salt.

3. Take a bowl and add breadcrumbs, parsley, lemon juice, zest, butter, and mix well.

4. Coat fillets with the breadcrumbs mixture and place fillets in your Air Crisping basket.

5. Lock Air Crisping lid and cook on Air Crisp mode for 15 minutes at 360 degrees F.

6. Serve and enjoy!

Nutrition:

- Calories: 231

- Fat: 20.1 g

- Saturated Fat: 2.4 g

- Carbohydrates: 20.1 g

- Fiber: 0.9 g

- Sodium: 941 mg

- Protein: 14.6 g

16.   Salmon Paprika

Preparation time: 5 min

Cooking time: 7 min **Servings:** 4

Ingredients:

- 2 wild-caught salmon fillets, 1 to 1 and ½ inches thick

- 2 teaspoons avocado oil 2 teaspoons paprika

- Salt and pepper to taste Green herbs to garnish

Directions:

1. Season salmon fillets with salt, pepper, paprika, and olive oil.

2. Place Crisping basket in your Ninja Foodi, and pre-heat your Ninja Foodie at 390 degrees F.

3. Place insert insider your Foodi, place the fillet in the insert, lock Air Crisping lid and cook for 7 minutes. Once done, serve the fish with herbs on top. Enjoy!

Nutrition:

- Calories: 231 Fat: 20.1 g Saturated Fat: 2.4 g

- Carbohydrates: 20.1 g Fiber: 0.9 g Sodium: 941 mg

- Protein: 14.6 g

CHAPTER 5:

Vegetable Recipes

17.   Cashew Stuffed Mushrooms

Preparation time: 10 minutes

Cooking time: 15 minutes

Servings: 6

Ingredients:

- 1 cup basil

- ½ cup cashew, soaked overnight

- ½ cup nutritional yeast

- 1 tablespoon lemon juice

- 2 cloves garlic

- 1 tablespoon olive oil

- Salt, to taste

- 1-pound (454 g) baby belle mushroom, stems removed

Directions:

1. Insert the Crisper Basket and close the hood. Select AIR CRISP, set the temperature to 400°F (204°C), and set the time to 15 minutes. Select START/STOP to begin preheating.

2. Prepare the pesto. In a food processor, blend the basil, cashew nuts, nutritional yeast, lemon juice, garlic, and olive oil to combine well. Sprinkle with salt, as desired.

3. Turn the mushrooms cap-side down and spread the pesto on the underside of each cap.

4. Transfer to the basket. Close the hood and AIR CRISP for 15 minutes.

5. Serve warm.

Nutrition:

- Calories: 200

- Fat: 12 g

- Carb: 16 g

- Proteins: 15 g

18.   Crusted Brussels Sprouts with Sage

Preparation time: 5 minutes

Cooking time: 15 minutes

Servings: 4

Ingredients:

- 1 lb. (454 g) Brussels sprouts, halved

- 1 cup bread crumbs

- 2 tbsp. Grana Padano cheese, grated

- 1 tbsp. paprika

- 2 tbsp. canola oil

- 1 tbsp. sage, chopped

Directions:

1. Line the Crisper Basket with parchment paper.

2. Insert the Crisper Basket and close the lid. Select ROAST, set the temperature to 400°F (204°C), and set the time to 15 minutes. Choose START/STOP to preheat.

3. In a small bowl, thoroughly mix the bread crumbs, cheese, and paprika. In a large bowl, place the Brussels sprouts and

drizzle the canola oil over the top. Sprinkle with the bread crumb mixture and toss to coat.

4. Place the Brussels sprouts in the Crisper Basket. Close the lie and ROAST for 15 minutes, or until the Brussels sprouts are lightly browned and crisp. Shake the basket a few times during cooking to ensure even cooking.

5. Transfer the Brussels sprouts to a plate and sprinkle the sage on top before serving.

Nutrition:

- Calories: 400

- Fat: 20 g.

- Saturated Fat: 10 g.

- Carbohydrates: 36 g.

- Fiber: 5 g.

- Sodium: 675 mg.

- Protein: 22 g.

CHAPTER 6:

Appetizers and Snacks Recipes

19.   Cabbage and Pork Gyoza

Preparation time: 10 minutes

Cooking time: 10 minutes per batch

Servings: 48 gyozas

Ingredients:

- 1-pound (454 g) ground pork

- 1 small head Napa cabbage (about 1 pound / 454 g), sliced thinly and minced

- ½ cup minced scallions

- 1 teaspoon minced fresh chives

- 1 teaspoon soy sauce

- 1 teaspoon minced fresh ginger

- 1 tablespoon minced garlic

- 1 teaspoon granulated sugar 2 teaspoons kosher salt

- 48 to 50 wonton or dumpling wrappers

- Cooking spray

Directions:

1. **Make the filling:** Combine all the ingredients, except for the wrappers in a large bowl. Stir to mix well.

2. Unfold a wrapper on a clean work surface, then dab the edges with a little water. Scoop up 2 teaspoons of the filling mixture in the center.

3. **Make the gyoza:** Fold the wrapper over to filling and press the edges to seal. Pleat the edges if desired. Repeat with remaining wrappers and fillings.

4. Spritz the Crisper Basket with cooking spray.

5. Insert the Crisper Basket and close the hood. Select AIR CRISP, set the temperature to 360°F (182°C), and set the time to 10 minutes. Select START/STOP to begin preheating.

6. Arrange the gyozas in the basket and spritz with cooking spray. Close the hood and AIR CRISP for 10 minutes or until golden brown. Flip the gyozas halfway through. Work in batches to avoid overcrowding.

7. Serve immediately.

Nutrition:

- Calories: 284 Carbs: 13 g

- Fat: 20 g Protein: 15 g

20.   Cheesy Potato Taquitos

Preparation time: 5 minutes

Cooking time: 6 minutes per batch

Servings: 12 taquitos

Ingredients:

- 2 cups mashed potatoes

- ½ cup shredded Mexican cheese

- 12 corn tortillas

- Cooking spray

Directions:

1. Select AIR CRISP, set the temperature to 400°F (204°C), and set the time to 6 minutes. Select START/STOP to begin preheating.

2. Line a baking pan with parchment paper.

3. In a bowl, combine the potatoes and cheese until well mixed. Microwave the tortillas on high heat for 30 seconds, or until softened. Add some water to another bowl and set alongside.

4. On a clean work surface, lay the tortillas. Scoop 3 tablespoons of the potato mixture in the center of each tortilla. Roll up tightly and secure with toothpicks if necessary.

5. Arrange the filled tortillas, seam side down, in the prepared baking pan. Spritz the tortillas with cooking spray.

6. Place the pan directly in the pot. Close the hood and AIR CRISP for 6 minutes, or until crispy and golden brown, flipping once halfway through the cooking time. You may need to work in batches to avoid overcrowding.

7. Serve hot.

Nutrition:

- Calories: 433

- Carbs: 55 g

- Fat: 14 g

- Protein: 21 g

21.   BLT with Grilled Heirloom Tomato

Preparation time: 10 minutes

Cooking time: 10 minutes

Servings: 4

Ingredients:

- 8 slices white bread

- 8 tbsp. mayonnaise

- 2 heirloom tomatoes, sliced 1/4-inch thick

- 2 tbsp. canola oil

- Sea salt to taste

- Freshly ground black pepper to taste

- 8 slices bacon, cooked

- 8 leaves iceberg lettuce

Directions:

1. Pull-out the Grill Grate, and adjacent the lid. Choice GRILL, set the temperature to MAX, and set the time to 10 minutes. Select START/STOP to begin preheating.

2. While the unit is preheating, spread a thin layer of mayonnaise on one side of each piece of bread.

3. When the unit toots to specify it has preheated, place the bread, mayonnaise-side down, on the Grill Grate. Close the lid and GRILL for 2–3 minutes, until crisp.

4. Meanwhile, remove the watery pulp and seeds from the tomato slices. Brush both sides of the tomatoes with oil and season with salt and pepper.

5. After 2–3 minutes, remove the bread and place the tomatoes on the grill. Close the lid and continue grilling for the remaining 6–8 minutes.

6. To accumulate, spread a thin layer of mayonnaise on the non-grilled sides of the bread. Layer the tomatoes, bacon, and lettuce on the bread, and top with the remaining slices of bread. Slice each sandwich in half and serve.

Nutrition:

- Calories: 103

- Carbohydrates: 11 g.

- Fat: 3.4 g.

- Protein: 0.9 g.

22.   Broccoli Bites

Preparation time: 5 minutes

Cooking time: 15 minutes

Servings: 3

Ingredients:

- 1/8 cup whole milk mozzarella cheese, grated

- 1 egg, beaten

- 1 cup broccoli florets

- Salt and black pepper to taste

- 3/4 cups feta cheese, grated

Directions:

1. Select the GRILL button on the Ninja Foodi Smart XL Grill and regulate MED settings for 15 minutes.

2. Pulse the broccoli with the rest of the ingredients in a food processor until crumbled finely.

3. Roll this mixture into equal-sized balls and refrigerate for at least 30 minutes.

4. Arrange the balls in the Ninja Foodi when it displays ADD FOOD.

5. Dole out on a plate when grilled completely and serve warm.

Serving suggestions: Sweet chili sauce will accompany these Broccoli Bites nicely.

Variation tip: Feta cheese can be replaced with ricotta cheese too.

Nutrition:

- Calories: 162
- Fat: 12.4 g.
- Sat Fat: 7.6 g.
- Carbohydrates: 1.9 g.
- Fiber: 0.5 g.
- Sugar: 0.9 g.
- Protein: 11.2 g.

23.   Rosemary and Baked Potatoes

Preparation time: 10 minutes.

Cooking time: 45–50 minutes.

Servings: 6

Ingredients:

- 1 tablespoon extra-virgin olive oil

- 2 teaspoons kosher salt

- 2 pounds of Yukon Gold, Red Bliss, or other thin-skinned potatoes (5–6 medium potatoes), scrubbed and clean

- 1 tablespoon dried rosemary or 2 tablespoons of minced fresh rosemary

Directions:

- Preheat the Ninja Foodi Smart XL to 425°F. Line a nonstick baking mat or a baking sheet with foil.

- Cut the potatoes into two and chop them into bite-sized pieces with the skins on. Then, transfer the potatoes to a large bowl and toss with the rosemary, olive oil, and salt. Make sure the potatoes are thoroughly coated with oil.

- Next spread the potatoes on the baking sheet. Then bake or cook for about 45 to 50 minutes until the potatoes become deeply golden; you should stir every 15 minutes. Serve.

Nutrition:

- **Energy (calories):** 100
- **Protein:** 1.88g
- **Fat:** 1.86g
- **Carbohydrates:** 21.57g

CHAPTER 7:

Desserts Recipes

24. Banana Fritter

Preparation time: 10 minutes

Cooking time: 15 minutes

Servings: 6

Ingredients:

- 1 medium butternut squash

- 2 teaspoons cumin seeds

- 1 large pinch of chili flakes

- 1 tablespoon olive oil

- 1- and 1/2-ounces pine nuts

- 1 small bunch of fresh coriander, chopped

Directions:

1. Pre-heat Ninja Foodi. Press the "AIR CRISP" option and set it to "340 Degrees F" and timer to 16 min

2. Take a bowl and add salt, sesame seeds, water and mix them well until a nice batter form

3. Coat the bananas with the flour mixture and transfer them to the Ninja Foodi Smart XL Grill Basket

4. Cook for 8 minutes

5. Enjoy!

Nutrition:

- Calories: 240

- Carbs: 30 g

- Fat: 10 g

Protein: 5 g

25.   Bloomin' Grilled Apples

Preparation time: 10 min.

Cooking time: 30 min

Servings: 4

Ingredients:

- 8 tbsp. maple cream caramel sauce, divided

- 4 scoops of vanilla ice cream

- 4 small baking apples

- 12 tsp. pecans, chopped, divided

Directions:

1. Press the GRILL button on the Ninja Foodi Smart XL Grill and adjust the time for 30 minutes.

2. Chop off the upper part of the apples and scoop the core out of the apples.

3. Cut the apple around the center and insert narrow cuts surrounding the apple.

4. Put the pecans and maple cream caramel sauce in the center of the apple.

5. Wrap the foil around the apple and put the apple inside the Ninja Foodi when it shows ADD FOOD.

6. Dish out in a platter and top with vanilla ice cream scoop to serve

Nutrition:

- Calories: 407

- Fat: 23 g.

- Saturated Fat: 12 g.

- Carbohydrates: 50 g.

- Fiber: 50 g.

- Sodium: 132 mg.

- Protein: 4 g.

26.　Cheese and Ham Stuffed Baby Bella

Preparation time: 15 minutes.

Cooking time: 12 minutes.

Servings: 8

Ingredients:

- 4 ounces (113 grams) Mozzarella cheese, cut into pieces

- ½ cup diced ham

- 2 green onions, chopped

- 2 tablespoons breadcrumbs

- ½ teaspoon garlic powder

- ¼ teaspoon ground oregano

- ¼ teaspoon ground black pepper

- 1 to 2 teaspoons olive oil

- 16 fresh Baby Bella mushrooms, stemmed removed

Directions:

- Process the cheese, ham, green onions, breadcrumbs, garlic powder, oregano, and pepper in a food processor until finely chopped.

- With the food processor running, carefully pour in 1 to 2 teaspoons olive oil until a thick paste has formed. Transfer the mixture to a bowl.

- Evenly divide the mixture into the mushroom caps and lightly press down the mixture.

- Insert the Crisper Basket and close the hood. Select bake, set the temperature to 390°F (199°C) and set the time to 12 minutes. Select start/stop to begin preheating.

- Lay the mushrooms in the Crisper Basket in a single layer. You'll need to work in batches to avoid overcrowding.

- Close the hood and bake for 12 minutes until the mushrooms are lightly browned and tender.

- Remove from the basket to a plate and repeat with the remaining mushrooms.

- Let the mushrooms cool for 5 minutes and serve warm.

Nutrition:

- Energy (calories): 105 Protein: 10.64g

- Fat: 1.63g Carbohydrates: 13.05g

27.   Nutella Cake

Preparation time: 10 minutes.

Cooking time: 25 minutes.

Servings: 2

Ingredients:

- 1 cup of sugar-free Nut-light

- 2 eggs, whisked

- 1/2 cup almond flour

- 6 raspberries, chopped

Directions:

- Take a bowl and then whisk eggs in it.

- Then add nut light and whisk well for a pleasing combination.

- Next, add flour to the mixture and finely incorporate it

- Grease the egg bites mold with oil.

- Divide the mixture between moulds.

- Top each meld with raspberries.

- Now pour 2 cups of water in Ninja Foodi.

- Place rack at the lower position of the Ninja Foodi Smart XL Grill.

- Put the egg mould on top of the rack—set pressure on high for 20 minutes.

- When the time completes, allow a natural release for 20 minutes. Remove the cake and put it on a baking rack for cooling.

- Return the cake to the Ninja Foodi smart XL and select bake.

- Cook or bake for 5 minutes at 400°F. Once done, serve.

Nutrition:

- **Calories:** 533

- **Fat:** 48.2g

- **Carbohydrate:** 8.7g

- **Protein:** 7.7g

CHAPTER 8:

Main Recipes

28.   Air Fried Lamb's Chops

Preparation time: 10 minutes

Cooking time: 5 Minutes

Servings: 3

Ingredients:

- 2.5 pounds of lamb chops

- Salt and black pepper to taste

- 1/2 cup Greek yogurt

- 4 tablespoons of honey

- Cayenne pepper to taste

Directions:

1. Cut the lamb chop into individual pieces to make individual lamb chop.

2. Season the chop with salt, black pepper.

3. Rub generously for fine coating.

4. Now rub the chops with cayenne pepper.

5. Drizzle honey over the lamb and baste it with a brush from both sides.

6. Season the lamb chops from both sides.

7. Now brush the chop with geek yogurt from both sides.

8. Now coat their fryer basket with oil spray.

9. Press air crisp set the temperature at 450 degrees and set a timer for 10 minutes for pre-heating.

10. Press start and let the Ninja Foodi pre-heated.

11. Now layer crisp airliner inside air crisp basket.

12. And place lamb chop in the basket and cook for 5 minutes inside the unit once pre-heating is done.

13. Once done, open Ninja Foodi and take-out lamb chops.

Nutrition:

- Calories940 % Daily Value*

- Total Fat 31.8 g 41%

- Saturated Fat 12.9 g 65%

- Cholesterol 350mg 117%

- Sodium 354mg 15%

- Total Carbohydrate 31.2 g 11%

- Dietary Fiber 0.1 g 0%

- Total Sugars 31.1 g Protein 126.4 g

29.   Delicious Donuts in Ninja Foodi Smart XL Grill

Preparation time: 5–10 minutes

Cooking time: 10 Minutes

Servings: 6

Ingredients:

- 1 1/2 cups sugar, powdered

- 1/3 cup whole milk

- 1/2 tsp. vanilla extract

- 16 oz. biscuit dough, prepared

- Oil spray for greasing

- 1 cup chocolate sprinkles for sprinkling

Directions:

1. Take a medium bowl and mix sugar, milk, and vanilla extract.

2. Combine well to create a glaze.

3. Set the glaze aside for further use.

4. Place the dough onto the flat, clean surface.

5. Flat the dough with a rolling pin.

6. Use a ring mold, about an inch, and cut the hole in each round dough's center.

7. Abode the dough on a plate and cool for 10 minutes.

8. Open the Ninja Foodi Grill and install the grill grate inside it.

9. Close the lid.

10. Now, select the Grill from the menu, and set the temperature to MED.

11. Set the time to 6 minutes.

12. Select start and begin preheating.

13. Remove the dough from the refrigerator and coat it with cooking spray from both sides.

14. When the unit beeps, the Grill is preheated; place the adjustable amount of dough on the grill grate.

15. Close the lid, and cook for 3 minutes.

16. After 3 minutes, remove donuts and place the remaining dough inside.

17. Cook for 3 minutes.

18. Once all the donuts are ready, sprinkle chocolate sprinkles on top.

19. Enjoy.

20. Remember to cool the donuts for 5 minutes before serving.

Nutrition:

- Calories: 400

- Fat: 11 g.

- Saturated Fat: 4.2 g.

- Cholesterol: 1 mg.

- Sodium: 787 mg.

- Carbohydrates: 71.3 g.

- Fiber 0.9 g.

- Sugar: 45.3 g

- Protein: 5.7 g.

30.   Frozen Barbecue Chicken Breasts

Preparation time: 5–10 minutes

Cooking time: 20 Minutes

Servings: 4

Ingredients:

- 4 (6-8 oz. each) chicken breasts, frozen, boneless, skinless

- 2 tbsp. canola oil, divided

- Kosher salt as desired

- Ground black pepper as desired

- 1 cup barbecue sauce, prepared

Directions:

1. The first step is to insert the grill grate inside the unit and close the lid.

2. Now, select the grill option and set the temperature to MED.

3. Set time to 20 minutes.

4. Now select start and begin the preheating process.

5. Meanwhile, brush each chicken piece with canola oil and season it with salt and black pepper.

6. Once the unit is preheated, place the chicken breast pieces onto the Grill and close the hood.

7. Cook it for 8 minutes.

8. Then open the Ninja Foodi and flip the chicken and cook for 6 minutes.

9. Next, open the Grill and baste the chicken with barbeque sauce from both sides.

10. Continue cooking for 6 minutes.

11. Once done, remove the chicken from the unit and let it sit for 5 minutes before cutting and serving.

12. Enjoy.

Nutrition:

- Calories: 41 Fat: 12.3 g.

- Saturated Fat: 2 g. Cholesterol: 131 mg.

- Sodium: 845 mg. Carbohydrates: 22.7 g.

- Fiber: 0.4 g.

- Sugar: 16.3 g.

- Protein: 49.3 g.

31. Chili-Rubbed Steak & Bread Salad

Preparation time: 10 minutes.

Cooking time: 15 minutes.

Servings: 8

Ingredients:

- 2 teaspoons chilli powder

- 1 beef top sirloin steak (1 inch thick and 1-1/4 pounds)

- 2 cups cubed multigrain bread 2 tablespoons olive oil

- 2 teaspoon brown sugar 1/2 teaspoon salt

- 1/2 teaspoon pepper

- 1 cup ranch salad dressing

- 2 tablespoons finely grated horseradish

- 1 medium cucumber, cut into 1-inch pieces

- 1 tablespoon prepared mustard

- 3 large tomatoes cut into 1-inch pieces

- 1 small red onion halved and thinly sliced

Directions:

- Combine chilli powder, brown sugar, salt, and pepper and rub
  it over steak. Let it stand for 15 minutes.

- Meanwhile, toss the bread cubes with oil. In a large skillet, toast bread over medium heat for 8–10 minutes or until crisp and lightly browned, stirring frequently. Take a small bowl, whisk salad dressing, horseradish, and mustard.

- Preheat the Ninja Foodi Smart XL Grill for 8 minutes before use. Grill steak while covered over medium heat or Broil. From heat 6 to 8 minutes on each side or until meat reaches desired doneness (for smart thermometer should read 135°F; medium, 140°F; medium-well, 145°F). Let stand for 5 minutes.

- Take a large bowl and mix cucumber, tomatoes, onions, and toasted bread. Add 1/2 cup dressing mixture and toss to coat. Slice steak; serve with salad and the remaining dressing.

Nutrition:

- **Calories:** 434

- **Fat:** 30g

- **Carbs:** 18g

- **Protein:** 23g

CHAPTER 9:

Sides Recipes

32.   Buffalo Chicken Meatballs

Preparation time: 10 minutes

Cooking time: 40 minutes

Servings: 6

Ingredients:

- 1-pound ground chicken

- 1 carrot, minced

- 2 celery stalks, minced

- ¼ cup crumbled blue cheese

- ¼ cup buffalo sauce

- ¼ cup breadcrumbs

- 1 egg

- 2 tablespoons extra-virgin olive oil

- ½ cup of water

Ingredients:

1. Choice Sear/Sauté and set it to high. Select Start/Stop to begin. Allow the pot to pre-heat for 5 minutes.

2. Meanwhile, in a large mixing bowl, mix the chicken, carrot, celery, blue cheese, buffalo sauce, breadcrumbs, and egg. Shape the mixture into 1½-inch meatballs.

3. Pour the olive oil into the preheated pot. Functioning in batches, place the meatballs in the pot and sear on all sides until browned. When each batch finishes catering, transfer to a plate.

4. Place the Cook & Crisp Basket in the pot. Add the water, then place all the meatballs in the basket.

5. Gather the Pressure Lid, making certain the pressure release valve is in the Seal position. Select Pressure and set to High. Fix the time to 5 minutes. Select Start/Stop to begin.

6. When pressure cooking is complete, quickly release the pressure by turning the pressure release valve to the vent position, carefully removing the lid when the unit has finished releasing pressure.

7. Adjust the Crisping Lid. Choice Air Crisp fixed the temperature to 360°F and set the time to 10 minutes. Select Start/Stop to begin.

8. After 5 minutes, open the lid, then lift the basket and shake the meatballs. Lesser the basket back into the pot and adjust the lid to resume cooking until the meatballs achieve your desired crispiness.

Nutrition:

- Calories: 204

- Total fat: 13 g

- Saturated fat: 4 g

- Cholesterol: 104 mg

- Sodium: 566 mg

- Carbohydrates: 5 g

- Fiber: 1 g

- Protein: 16 g

33.　　Citrus Carrots

Preparation time: 10 minutes

Cooking time: 22 minutes

Servings: 4

Ingredients:

- 2 tsp. fresh ginger, minced

- 2 tsp. olive oil

- 3 cups carrots, peeled and sliced

- Salt and black pepper to taste

- 1/2 cup fresh orange juice

Directions:

1. Select the GRILL button on the Ninja Foodi Smart XL Grill and regulate MED settings for 10 minutes.

2. Mingle the carrots with all other ingredients in a bowl.

3. Arrange the carrots in the Ninja Foodi when it displays "ADD FOOD".

4. Grill for 10 minutes, stirring once in between.

5. Dole out on a plate when grilled completely and serve warm.

Serving suggestions: Serve Citrus Carrots over a bed of rice.

Variation tip: use fresh carrots.

Nutrition:

- Calories: 111

- Fat: 6.6 g.

- Sat. Fat: 0.8 g.

- Carbohydrates: 12 g.

- Fiber: 2.2 g.

- Sugar: 6.7 g.

- Protein: 1 g.

CHAPTER 10:

Poultry Recipes

34.   Crispy Chicken Strips

Preparation time: 15 minutes

Cooking time: 20 minutes

Servings: 4

Ingredients:

- 1 tablespoon olive oil

- 1 pound (454 g) boneless, skinless chicken tenderloins

- 1 teaspoon salt

- ½ teaspoon freshly ground black pepper

- ½ teaspoon paprika

- ½ teaspoon garlic powder

- ½ cup whole-wheat seasoned breadcrumbs

- 1 teaspoon dried parsley

- Cooking spray

Directions:

1. Spray the Crisper Basket lightly with cooking spray.

2. Insert the Crisper Basket and close the hood. Select AIR CRISP, set the temperature to 370°F (188°C), and set the time to 20 minutes. Select START/STOP to begin preheating.

3. In a medium bowl, toss the chicken with the salt, pepper, paprika, and garlic powder until evenly coated.

4. Add the olive oil and toss to coat the chicken evenly.

5. In a separate, shallow bowl, mix together the breadcrumbs and parsley.

6. Coat each piece of chicken evenly in the bread crumb mixture.

7. Place the chicken in the Crisper Basket in a single layer and spray it lightly with cooking spray. You may need to cook them in batches.

8. Close the hood and AIR CRISP for 10 minutes. Flip the chicken over, lightly spray it with cooking spray, and AIR CRISP for an additional 8 to 10 minutes, until golden brown. Serve.

Nutrition:

- Calories: 374

- Fat: 8 g

- Carb: 34 g

- Proteins: 37 g

35.   Garlic Chicken Potatoes

Preparation time: 10 minutes.

Cooking time: 30 minutes.

Servings: 4

Ingredients:

- 2 pounds (907.185 grams) red potatoes, quartered

- 2 tablespoons olive oil

- 1/2 teaspoon cumin seeds

- Salt and black pepper to taste

- 2 garlic cloves, chopped

- 2 tablespoons brown sugar

- 1 lemon (1/2 juiced and 1/2 cut into wedges)

- Pinch of red pepper flakes

- 1 pound skinless, boneless chicken breasts

- 2 tablespoons cilantro, chopped

Directions:

- Place the chicken, lemon, garlic, and potatoes in a baking pan.

- Toss the spices, herbs, oil, and sugar in a bowl.

- Add this mixture to the chicken and veggies, then toss well to coat.

- Press the "power button" of Ninja Foodi Smart XL Grill and select the "bake" mode.

- Press the time button and set the cooking time to 30 minutes.

- Now push the temp button and set the temperature to 400°F.

- When it is preheated, place the baking pan inside and close its lid.

- Serve warm.

Nutrition:

- Calories: 545

- Fat: 36.4g

- Carbs: 40.7g

- Fibre: 0.2g

- Protein: 42.5g

36.   Ninja Foodi Fried Chicken with Smashed Potatoes and Corn

Preparation Time: 10 minutes **Cooking Time:** 25 minutes

Servings: 4

Ingredients;

- 4 bone-in, skin-on chicken thighs 2 tsp. kosher salt or 1 tsp. fine salt, divided 1 cup Bisquick or similar baking mix

- ½ cup unsalted butter, melted, divided

Directions:

1. Sprinkle the chicken with 1 tsp. of kosher salt. Place the baking mix in a prepared shallow dish. Brush the thighs on all sides with ¼ cup of butter, and then dredge them in the baking mixture, coating them all on sides. Arrange the chicken in the center of the sheet pan.

2. Place the potatoes in a prepared large bowl with 2 tbsp. of butter and toss to coat. Place them on the side of the chicken arranged on the pan.

3. Place the corn in a Medium bowl and drizzle with the remaining 2 tbsp. of butter. Sprinkle with ¼ tsp. of kosher

salt and toss to coat. Place on the pan on the other side of the chicken.

4. Select Roast, on Ninja Foodi Smart and set the temperature to 375 °F., and set time to 25 minutes. select Start/stop to

5. Once the unit has preheated, slide the pan into the oven.

6. After 20 minutes, just remove the pan from the Ninja Foodi Smart and transfer the potatoes back to the bowl. Return the pan to Ninja Foodi Smart XL and continue cooking.

7. As the chicken continues cooking, add the cream, black pepper, and remaining ¾ tsp. of kosher salt to the potatoes. Lightly mash the potatoes by using a potato masher or fork.

8. When cooking is completed, the corn will be tender and the chicken cooked through, reading 165 °F. on a meat thermometer. Remove the pan from the Ninja Foodi Smart and serve the chicken with the mashed potatoes and corn on the side.

Nutrition:

- Calories: 763 Fat: 55 g Carbohydrates: 48 g

- Fibre: 4 g Protein: 24 g

37. Turkey Burgers with Cheddar and Roasted Onions

Preparation Time: 10 minutes **Cooking Time:** 10 minutes

Servings: 4

Ingredients:

- 2 Medium yellow or white onions

- 1 tbsp. extra-virgin olive oil or vegetable oil

- 1½ tsp. Kosher salt or ¾ tsp. fine salt, divided

- 1¼ pound ground turkey

- 1/3 cup mayonnaise

- 1 tbsp. Dijon mustard

- 2 tsp. Worcestershire sauce

- 4 slices sharp cheddar cheese (about 4 ounces total)

- 4 hamburger buns, sliced

Directions:

1. Cut the onions in half through the root. Cut one of the halves in half (so you have a quarter). Grate one quarter. Place the grated onion in a large bowl. Thinly slice the remaining onions and place in a Medium bowl with the oil and ½ tsp. of kosher

salt. Toss to coat. Place the onions on the sheet pan in a single layer.

2. Select Roast mode on Ninja Foodi, set temperature to 350 °F., and set time to 10 minutes. Select Start/stop to begin preheating.

3. Once the unit has preheated, slide the pan into the oven.

4. While the onions are cooking, add the turkey to the grated onion. Add the remaining 1 tsp of kosher salt, mayonnaise, mustard, and Worcestershire sauce. Mix just until combined, and be careful not to overcook the turkey. Divide the mixture into four patties, each about ¾-inch thick.

5. When cooking is complete, just remove the pan from the oven. Transfer the onions to one side of the pan and place the burgers on the pan. Press your finger into the center of each burger to make a deep indentation (this helps the burgers cook evenly).

6. Select Broil, set temperature to high, and set time to 12 minutes. Select Start/stop to begin preheating.

7. Once preheated, slide the pan into the oven. After 6 minutes, remove the pan. Turn the burgers and stir the onions. (If the

onions are getting charred, transfer them to a bowl and cover with foil.)

8. Return the pan to Ninja Foodi Smart XL and continue cooking. After about 4 minutes, remove the pan and place the cheese slices on the burgers. Return the pan to the range, continue cooking for about 1 minute, or until the cheese is melted and the center of the burgers has reached at least 160 °F. on a meat thermometer.

9. When cooking is completed, just remove the pan from the oven. Loosely cover the burgers with foil.

10. Layout the buns, cut-side up, on the oven rack. Select Broil; set temperature to high, and set time to 3 minutes. Select Start/stop to begin. Check the buns after 2 minutes; they should be lightly browned.

11. Remove the buns from the oven. Assemble the burgers and add any condiments you like.

Nutrition:

- Calories: 579 Fat: 33 g Carbohydrates: 32 g
- Fibre: 2 g Protein: 36 g

38.   Bacon-Wrapped Turkey Tenderloins

with Honey Balsamic Carrots

Preparation Time: 10 minutes

Cooking Time: 25 minutes

Servings: 4

Ingredients:

- 2 oz. turkey tenderloins

- 1 tsp. Kosher salt or ½ tsp. fine salt, divided

- 6 slices bacon (not thick cut)

- 3 tbsp. Balsamic vinegar

- 1 tbsp. Dijon mustard

- ½ tsp. dried thyme

- 6 large carrots, peeled and cut into ¼-inch rounds

- 1 tbsp. extra-virgin olive oil

- 2 tbsp. Honey

Directions:

1. Sprinkle the turkey with ¾ tsp. of the salt (if your tenderloins are brined, omit this step). Wrap each tenderloin with three

strips of bacon, securing the bacon with toothpicks if necessary. Place the turkey on the sheet pan.

2. In a prepared small bowl, mix the balsamic vinegar, honey, mustard, and thyme.

3. Place the carrots in a Medium bowl and drizzle with the oil. Add 1 tbsp. of the balsamic mixture and ¼ tsp. of kosher salt and toss to coat. Place them on the pan around the turkey tenderloins. Baste the tenderloins with about one-half of the remaining balsamic mixture.

4. Select Roast on Ninja Foodi Smart, set temperature to 375 °F., and set time to 25 minutes. Select Start/stop to begin preheating.

5. Once the Ninja Foodi Smart XL has preheated, slide the pan into the oven.

6. After 13 minutes, just remove the pan from the oven. Gently stir the carrots. Turn over the tenderloins and baste them with the remaining balsamic mixture. Return the pan to the Ninja Foodi and continue cooking.

7. When cooking is completed, the carrots should be tender, and the center of the tenderloins should register 155 °F. on a meat

thermometer (the temperature will continue to rise). Remove the pan from the oven. Slice the turkey and serve with the carrots.

Nutrition:

- Calories: 462

- Fat: 19 g

- Carbohydrates: 20 g

- Fibre: 3 g

- Protein: 51 g

39.　　Maple-Glazed Chicken Wings

Preparation Time: 5 minutes

Cooking Time: 14 minutes

Servings: 4

Ingredients:

- 1 cup maple syrup

- 1/3 cup soy sauce

- ¼ cup teriyaki sauce

- Three garlic cloves, minced

- 2 tsp. garlic powder

- 2 tsp. onion powder

- 1 tsp. freshly ground black pepper

- 2 pounds bone-in chicken wings (drumettes and flats)

Directions:

1. Put inside the grill grate and close the hood. Select Grill, set the temperature to Medium, and set the time to 14 minutes. Select Start/stop to begin preheating.

2. In the meantime, in a large bowl, whisk together the maple syrup, soy sauce, teriyaki sauce, garlic powder, garlic, onion

powder, and black pepper. Add the wings, and use tongs to toss and coat.

3. When the Ninja Foodi Smart XL beeps, it has preheated, then place the chicken wings on the grill grate. Close the lid and then cook for at least 5 minutes. After 5 minutes, flip the wings, close the hood, and cook for an additional 5 minutes.

4. Check the wings for doneness. It is completely cooked when the internal temperature of the meat reaches at least 165 °F. on a food thermometer. If needed, cook for up to 4 minutes more.

5. Remove from the grill and serve.

Variation Tip: Spice up this maple-glazed wing recipe by adding ¼ tsp. red pepper flakes to the maple syrup mixture.

Nutrition:

- Calories: 722 Fat: 36 g
- Carbohydrates: 59 g
- Fibre: 1 g
- Protein: 41 g

40.   Breaded Chicken Piccata

Preparation Time: 5 minutes

Cooking Time: 22 minutes

Servings: 4

Ingredients:

- 2 large eggs

- ½ cup all-purpose flour

- ½ tsp. freshly ground black pepper

- 2 boneless, skinless chicken breasts

- 4 tbsp. Unsalted butter

- 1 lemon juice 1 tbsp. capers, drained

Directions:

1. Insert the Crisper Basket and close the hood. Select Air Crisp, set the temperature to 375 °F. and set the time to 22 minutes. Select Start/stop to begin preheating.

2. Meanwhile, in a medium shallow bowl, whisk the eggs until they are thoroughly beaten.

3. In a separate medium shallow bowl, combine the flour and black pepper, using a fork to distribute the pepper evenly.

4. Pour the chicken in the flour to coat it thoroughly, then dip it into the egg, then back in the flour.

5. When the Ninja Foodi Smart XL beeps, it has preheated, then place the chicken in the basket. Close the hood and cook for 18 minutes.

6. While the chicken is cooking, melt the butter in a skillet over Medium heat. Add the lemon juice and capers, and bring to a simmer. Reduce the heat to Low, and simmer for 4 minutes.

7. After 18 minutes, check the chicken. It is completely cooked when the internal temperature of the meat reaches at least 165 °F. on a food thermometer. If necessary, close the hood and continue cooking for up to 3 minutes more.

8. Arrange the chicken on a plate, and drizzle the butter sauce over each serving.

Nutrition:

- Calories: 522 Fat: 30 g Carbohydrates: 28 g

- Fibre: 1 g Protein: 36 g

Conclusion

With the Ninja Foodie XL Grill Cookbook, you'll learn how to prepare the freshest food any way you like. You'll start with the basics and work your way up to more advanced techniques. With each technique, you'll get step-by-step instructions and helpful hints to make sure your foods turn out just right. Final Ninja Foodie XL Grill Tips:

- If you're new to grilling, start with the basics—the recipes are written for someone with minimal grilling experience.
- If you're a more advanced griller, feel free to use the recipes as a guide and make your own modifications.
- When you're grilling, always keep in mind that safety is the most important thing—if it seems like a recipe may be too complicated or you're not in a position to grill safely, then don't.
- Remember to grill in moderation and always have plenty of water on hand.
- Don't underestimate your Ninja Foodie XL Grill, especially when grilling.
- Have fun and enjoy the summer!

Tired of bland, boring grilled food? The Ninja Foodie XL Grill Cookbook is the perfect way to kickstart your grilling abilities. With great teaching tools like photos with every recipe and a large variety of recipes that range from basic to advanced and everything in between, you'll be well on your way to becoming a ninja griller.

If you own a Ninja Foodie XL Grill Cookbook, then you already know that it's more than just a grill cookbook. You've probably used it in ways that we never imagined. For instance, you may have used it to make "kabobs" by simply placing the meat on a skewer and cooking it on the grill. That's right! You just placed the meat on a skewer and cooked it!

But there's even more to the Ninja Foodie XL Grill Cookbook than this. You can use the cookbook to start your restaurant using your Ninja Foodie XL Grill Cookbook as a menu. You can even make food for customers right in your kitchen and then have them take it back to their homes with their own Ninja Foodie XL Grill Cookbook. This grill is for everyone no matter if he/she is a professional chef or a person who has just started to cook and wants to cook healthy food with no artificial preservatives added. Ninja Foodi Smart XL Grill is easy to use and will help you prepare your favorite recipes in minutes. It will inspire you to try new recipes as well. This grill comes with an excellent customer support service that will answer any question you might have within 24 hours. A smart grill that promises to cook food faster which is safer and healthier, enter the world of technology. From the name itself, Ninja Foodi Smart XL Grill is a grill that is smart and promises convenient for everyone to use. With this grill, it claims to cook meat in a healthy manner by emitting infrared heat from its dome-shaped lid. It sizzles the meat while leaving moisture and then results in a juicy flavor.

You can also use your Ninja Foodie XL Grill Cookbook to barbecue animals such as turkeys, chickens, and ducks on your grill. And you can roast marshmallows on your grill using your Ninja Foodie XL Grill Cookbook. You'll find all the Ninja Foodie XL Grill Cookbook tools that are necessary to do so inside of this cookbook! In conclusion, if you own a Ninja Foodie XL Grill Cookbook, then you'll see that it's more than just a grill cookbook; it's a tool that will allow you to experience many cooking techniques that we could never have imagined!

CPSIA information can be obtained
at www.ICGtesting.com
Printed in the USA
BVHW091152270521
608294BV00003B/446

9 781801 824101